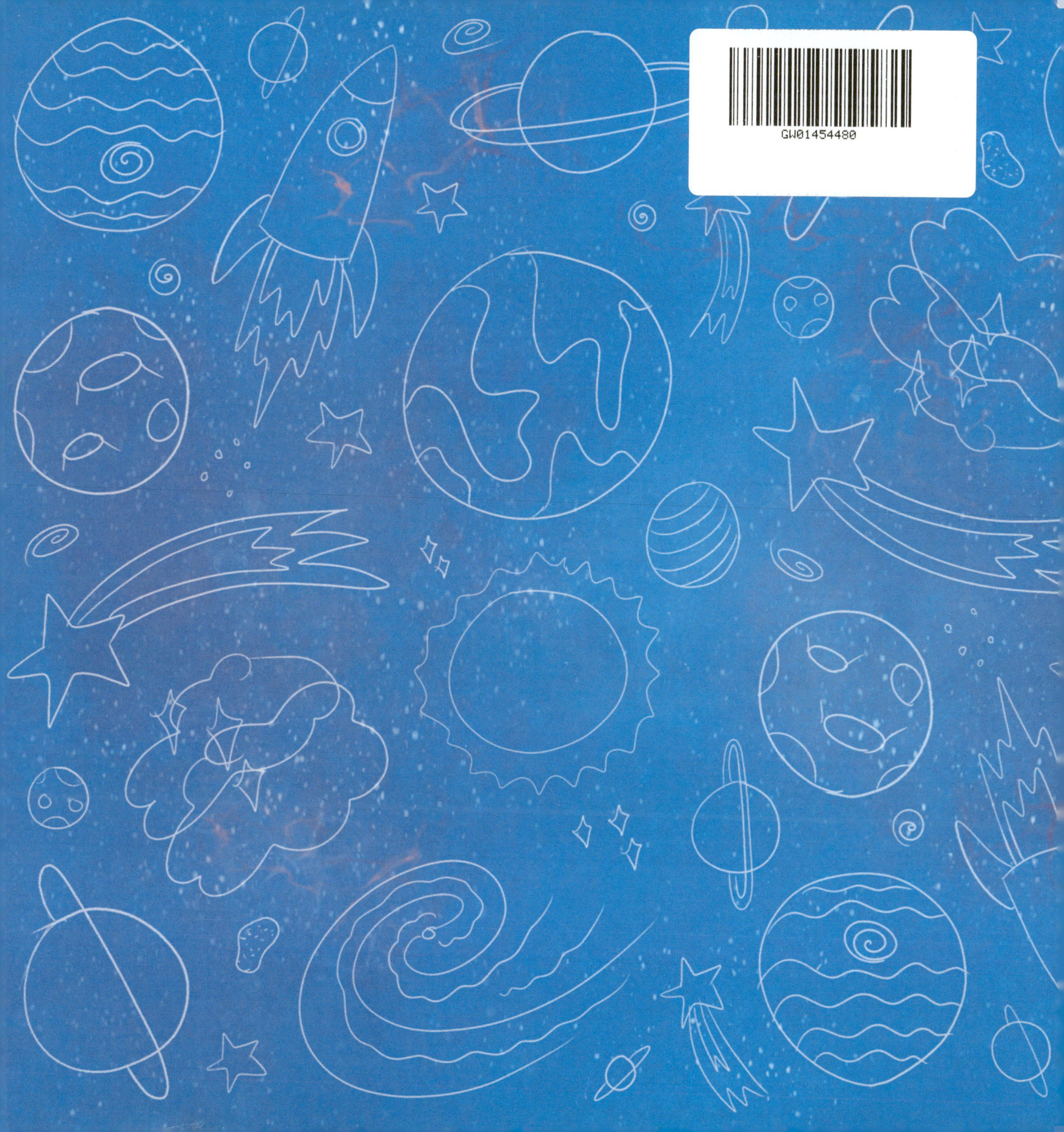

Let's Take a Look at

The Solar System

By Sara Lloyd

For Daniel

May your curiosity know no bounds

Our solar system is a dazzling place:

Eight planets orbiting in outer space.

With satellites, rockets and robotic space probes,

We've explored just a little of what's beyond our globe.

Let's take a look!

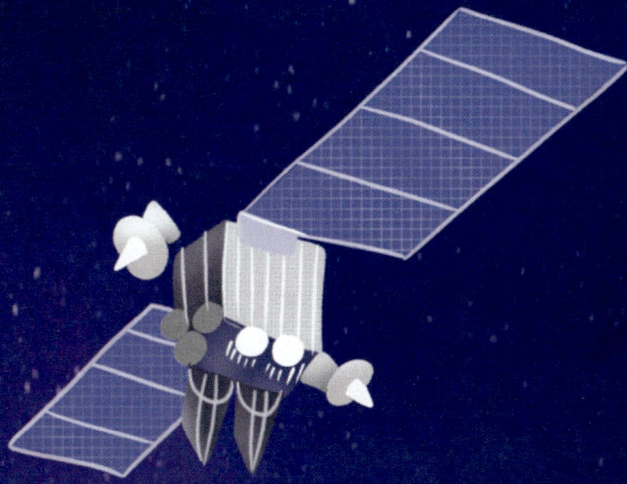

At the centre, the Sun is where we begin.

The planets move round it as they spin.

Not a planet itself, the Sun is a star,

The largest body in the system by far.

Although it seems huge with its fiery glare,

This star is quite small next to others out there,

But in our solar system, living creatures survive

While the Sun's light and warmth keep us alive.

The first planet, Mercury, is a small, rocky place.

Craters cover its wrinkly face.

When asteroids or comets with its surface collide,

Some holes measure over a kilometre wide.

Mercury is the quickest to orbit the sun;

In 88 days, its year is done.

While its surface looks rocky, beneath there is more;

At the heart of this planet is a molten core.

Next we have Venus, like a jewel set alight.

We can see it from Earth on a very clear night.

Venus spins round on its axis sideways.

Unlike Earth, it turns round the opposite way.

There are countless volcanoes and some still explode

In incredibly long, scorching, hot lava flows.

Acid filled clouds swarm the atmosphere,

Making Venus the hottest of the system's eight spheres.

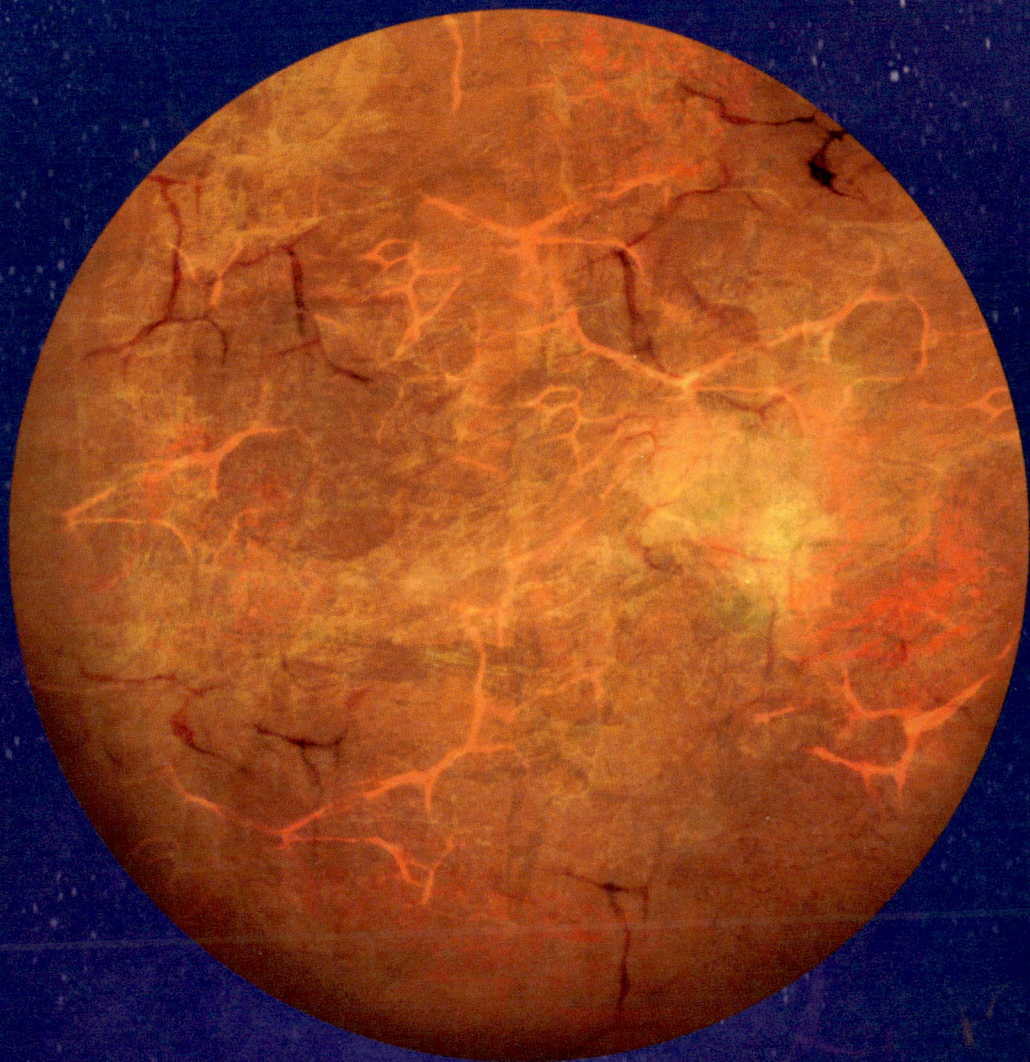

The third planet, Earth, is the one we call home.

It is perfectly formed for life to roam.

The surface is made up of both land and sea.

There is one moon in the sky we can see.

The landscape is varied with mountains and lakes,

Volcanoes and deserts, fjords and earthquakes.

From the clouds up above come hail, sleet and snow,

And showers of rain causing green plants to grow.

Mars is a cold, desert planet of dust.

The surface looks red because of the rust

That covers the rocks and soil on the ground.

There are two moons in orbit around.

Less gravity on Mars makes objects feel light.

If you landed here you could jump three times the height!

Both valleys and mountains make up its terrain.

'Olympus Mons' is the tallest peak's name.

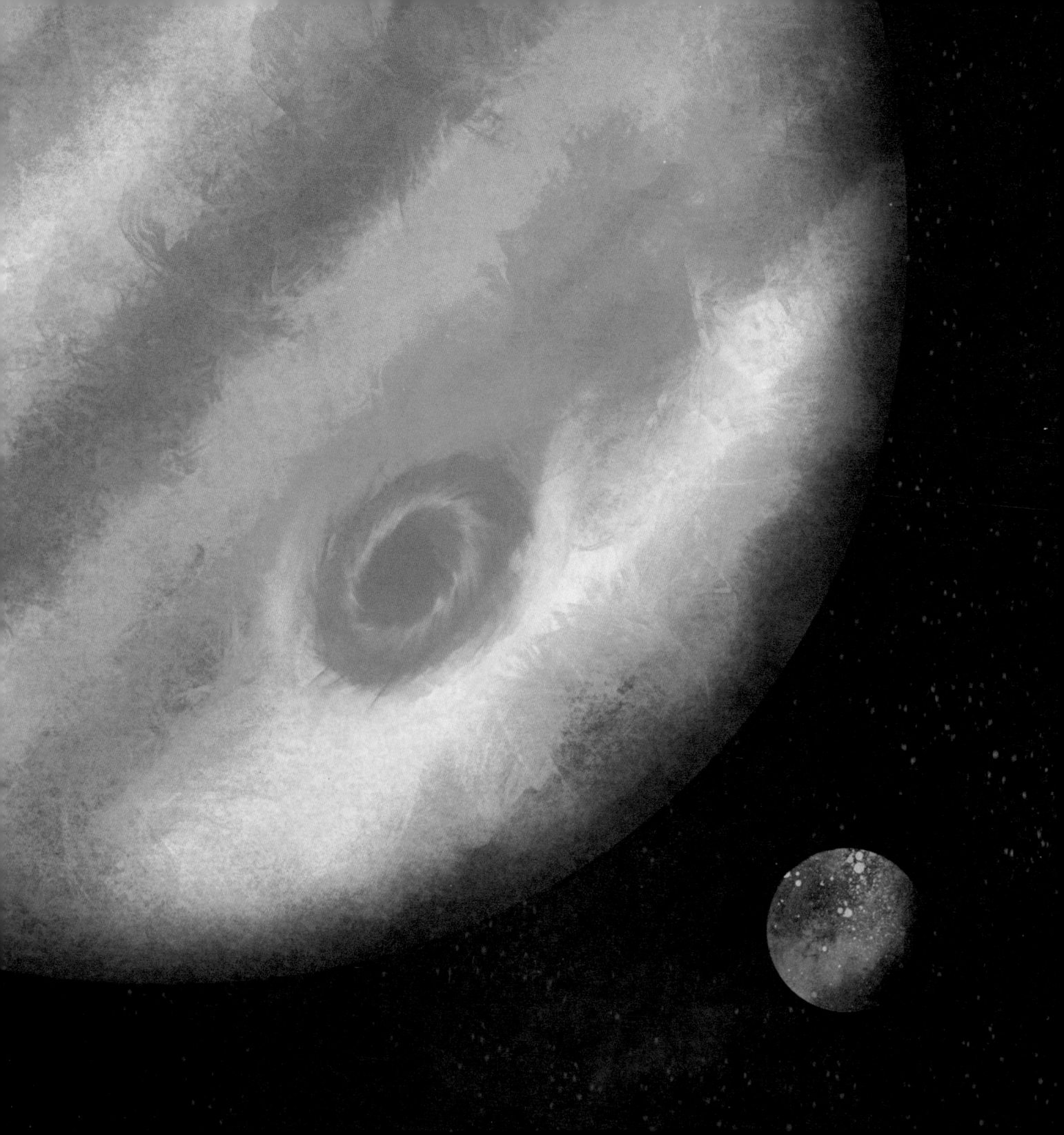

Next up is Jupiter, a giant of gas.

No other planet spins round as fast.

Its magnetic field is the strongest too;

One step onto Jupiter would squash you!

We can see a huge red spot on its side

Where a powerful storm is raging inside.

With 68 moons above its cloud cover,

Scientists think there are more to discover.

With its broad rings, Saturn is stunning to see:

A planet of unrivalled, cosmic beauty.

Ice, rocks and dust form the rings going round.

Its surface is gas rather than solid ground.

The second largest planet to orbit our star,

It has even more moons than Jupiter.

Saturn is so light that if it were a boat,

We could set it on an ocean and it would float.

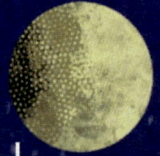

The seventh planet is Uranus, cold and stark.

It rotates on its side, so half remains in the dark

For 42 Earth years; What a long winter time!

The planet's gas and ice creates a brilliant, blue shine

Neptune is the eighth and final planet on our tour.

The strongest of winds rage in Neptune's storms.

An icy world of mystery, of darkness and cold,

On this harsh and hostile planet, no life can take hold.

Where our solar system ends, space has only just begun;

A billion, sparkling galaxies stretch out on and on.

While we keep on exploring, we may never see it all.

The size of the whole universe is astronomical!

It is easy to feel small when we look at space above,

But we are all unique and special,

Made to fill the world with love.

Manufactured by Amazon.com.au
Sydney, New South Wales, Australia